Gabriel Jackson

MISSA SANCTAE MARGARETAE

MUSIC DEPARTMENT

OXFORD
UNIVERSITY PRESS

OXFORD
UNIVERSITY PRESS

Great Clarendon Street, Oxford OX2 6DP, England

Oxford University Press is a department of the University of Oxford.
It furthers the University's aim of excellence in research, scholarship,
and education by publishing worldwide in

Oxford New York
Auckland Bangkok Buenos Aires Cape Town Chennai
Dar es Salaam Delhi Hong Kong Istanbul Karachi Kolkata
Kuala Lumpur Madrid Melbourne Mexico City Mumbai Nairobi
São Paulo Shanghai Taipei Tokyo Toronto

Oxford is a registered trade mark of Oxford University Press
in the UK and in certain other countries

7 9 10 8 6

ISBN 978-0-19-337755-4

Printed in Great Britain on acid-free paper by
Halstan & Co. Ltd, Amersham, Bucks.

CONTENTS

Duration: 12 minutes

TEXTS AND TRANSLATIONS

These texts and translations may be reproduced as required for programme notes.

KYRIE

Kyrie eleison.
Christe eleison.
Kyrie eleison.

Lord have mercy.
Christ have mercy.
Lord have mercy.

GLORIA

Gloria in excelsis Deo
et in terra pax hominibus bonae voluntatis.
Laudamus te.
Benedicimus te.
Adoramus te.
Glorificamus te.
Gratias agimus tibi propter magnam gloriam tuam.
Domine Deus,
Rex caelestis,
Deus Pater omnipotens.
Domine Fili unigenite, Jesu Christe.
Domine Deus, Agnus Dei, Filius Patris.
Qui tollis peccata mundi, miserere nobis.
Qui tollis peccata mundi, suscipe deprecationem nostram.
Qui sedes ad dexteram Patris, miserere nobis.
Quoniam tu solus Sanctus,
tu solus Dominus,
tu solus Altissimus, Jesu Christe.
Cum Sancto Spiritu in gloria Dei Patris.
Amen.

Glory to God in the highest
and on earth peace to men of goodwill.
We praise you.
We bless you.
We adore you.
We glorify you.
We give you thanks for your great glory.
Lord God,
Heavenly King,
God the Father almighty.
Lord the only-begotten son, Jesus Christ.
Lord God, Lamb of God, Son of the Father.
Who takes away the sins of the world, have mercy on us.
Who takes away the sins of the world, receive our prayer.
Who sits at the right hand of the Father, have mercy on us.
For you only are holy,
you alone are Lord,
you alone are the most high, Jesus Christ.
With the Holy Spirit in the Glory of God the Father.
Amen.

SANCTUS & BENEDICTUS

Sanctus, sanctus, sanctus,
Dominus Deus Sabaoth.
Pleni sunt caeli et terra gloria tua.
Hosanna in excelsis.

Holy, holy, holy.
Lord God of Sabaoth.
Heaven and earth are full of your glory.
Hosanna in the highest.

Benedictus qui venit in nomine Domini:
Hosanna in excelsis.

Blessed is he who comes in the name of the Lord:
Hosanna in the highest.

AGNUS DEI

Agnus Dei, qui tollis peccata mundi: miserere nobis.
Agnus Dei, qui tollis peccata mundi: miserere nobis.
Agnus Dei, qui tollis peccata mundi: dona nobis pacem.

Lamb of God, who takes away the sins of the world: have mercy on us.
Lamb of God, who takes away the sins of the world: have mercy on us.
Lamb of God, who takes away the sins of the world: give us peace.

Missa Sanctae Margaretae

GABRIEL JACKSON

KYRIE

Duration: 12'

First performed by the choir of St Margaret's Church, Oxford, directed by Richard Goodall, on 18 July 2010.

6

GLORIA

SANCTUS & BENEDICTUS

24

AGNUS DEI

Brockley, February–May 2010